YOU CALL THAT A NOSE?

Learning About Human Senses with

THE GARBAGE GANG

by Thomas Kingsley Troupe

illustrated by Derek Toye

PICTURE WINDOW BOOKS
a capstone imprint

MEET THE GARBAGE GANG:

SAM HAMMWICH

Sam is a once-delicious sandwich that has a bit of lettuce and tomato. He is usually crabby and a bit of a loudmouth.

GORDY

Gordy is a small rhino who wears an eyepatch even though he doesn't need one. He lives in the city dump. His friends don't visit him in the smelly dump, so Gordy created his own friends—the Garbage Gang!

SOGGY

Soggy is a stuffed bear from a carnival game. She fell into a puddle of dumpster juice and has never been the same.

RICK

Rick is a brick. He is terrified of bugs, especially bees, which is odd ... since he's a brick.

CANN-DEE

Cann-Dee is a robot made of aluminum cans. She can pull random facts out of thin air.

MR. FRIGID

Mr. Frigid is a huge refrigerator that sprouted arms and legs. He doesn't say much, but he's super strong.

We can help you, Ella. Where did you last see your dad? Do you know which direction?

I don't.

What were you guys doing at the dump? Most people don't like to come out here.

Yeah, the dump stinks!

My dad needed to get rid of some tree branches. He drives a blue truck.

Well, if we never find him, you can come live at Gordy's house.

Yeah, and tonight is taco night!

I sure like tacos, but I couldn't live here. I'd miss my family too much.

Don't worry, Ella. We'll find your dad.

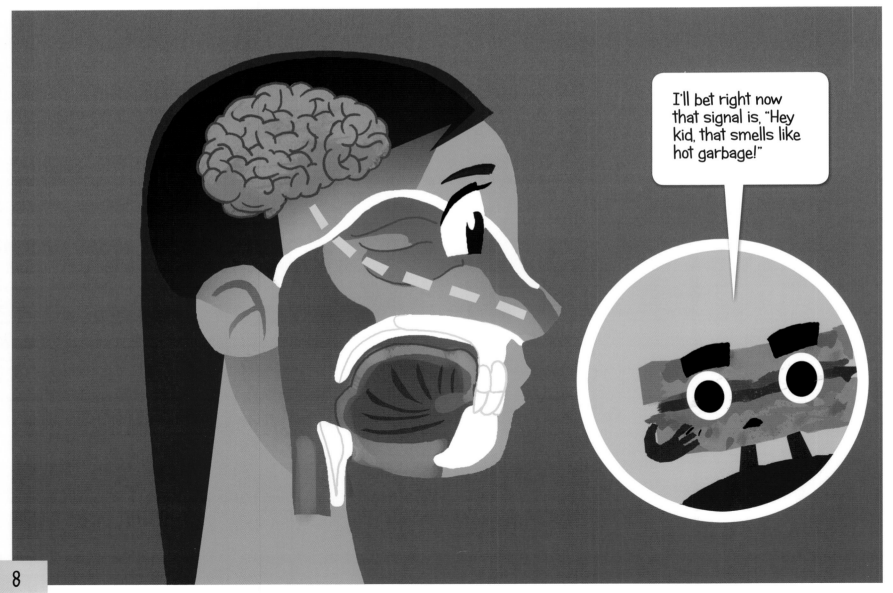

So, if that weird looking thing on your face smells stuff, how do you taste things?

That's what my tongue is for.

Whoa! Put that back!

It looks like a little red snake.

Calm down, guys. I have one too!

Boy, humans and animals are gross.

Not really. We have cool body parts that help us sense things. The tongue is super helpful.

How does it work?

When I eat stuff, food gets on my tongue. My tongue's taste buds send a signal ...

Let me guess ... to your brain?

That's right. Taste buds tell my brain that something is sweet, sour, bitter, or salty. If my brain doesn't like the taste ...

You could spit it out?

I was going to ask what those silly things on the side of your head are.

Be nice, Sam.

It's OK. Ears are kind of funny looking.

The ear is built to capture sound waves.

Whoa, like a catcher's mitt?

Sort of. The sound waves go into my ear, and a nerve signal travels to my brain. From the signal, my brain hears a sound. My brain can tell what the sound is and how far away it is. Sometimes my ear can even tell where the sound is coming from.

With all these senses, there's no way we can't find your dad.

Let's all be quiet for a second. Maybe we can hear my dad calling.

ELLAᴀᴀ

Holy buckets! I can hear him!

Awesome! Can you tell where he is?

I can't. There's too much other noise. Let's get to Mount Trash ... and fast!

15

To the brain. We know, we know.

Yes, seeing what's out there is really helpful. Sight helps me find things, stay out of danger, and see cool things.

Like your dad?

Well ... yeah!

17

Glossary

ability—the skill to do something

exhaust—waste gases from an engine

mechanical—working parts of a machine

sense—a way of knowing about your surroundings; hearing, smelling, touching, tasting, and seeing are the five senses

sensor—a device used to detect sound, movement, or light

signal—a message between our brains and our senses

You're looking up words? That's one smart move, kid!

Read More

Lay, Kathryn. *Smelling Their Prey: Animals with an Amazing Sense of Smell*. Sensing Their Prey. Minneapolis: Magic Wagon, 2013.

Stewart, Melissa. *How Does the Ear Hear?: And Other Questions About the Five Senses*. New York: Sterling Children's Books, 2014.

Townsend, John. *Amazing Animal Senses*. Animal Superpowers. Chicago: Raintree, 2013.

Incoming data suggests that books don't stink.

Critical Thinking Using the Common Core

1. Name the five human senses. Which senses are you using right now? (Key Ideas and Details)

2. Senses can help keep us safe. Name two ways senses do this. (Integration of Knowledge and Ideas)

Index

Internet Sites

FactHound offers a safe, fun way to find Internet sites related to this book. All of the sites on FactHound have been researched by our staff.

Here's all you do:

Visit www.facthound.com

Type in this code: 9781479570584

Super-cool stuff! Check out projects, games and lots more at www.capstonekids.com

Thanks to our adviser for his expertise, research, and advice:
Christopher T. Ruhland, PhD
Professor of Biological Sciences
Department of Biology
Minnesota State University, Mankato

Editor: Shelly Lyons
Designer: Aruna Rangarajan
Creative Director: Nathan Gassman
Production Specialist: Lori Barbeau
The illustrations in this book were created digitally
Picture Window Books are published by Capstone,
1710 Roe Crest Drive, North Mankato, Minnesota 56003
www.capstonepub.com

Library of Congress Cataloging-in-Publication Data
Troupe, Thomas Kingsley, author.
You call that a nose? : learning about human senses with the Garbage Gang / by Thomas Kingsley Troupe.
pages cm. — (Picture Window books. The Garbage Gang's super science questions)
Summary: "Humorous text and characters help teach kids about human senses"— Provided by publisher.
Audience: Ages 5-7
Audience: K to grade 3
Includes bibliographical references and index.
ISBN 978-1-4795-7058-4 (library binding)
ISBN 978-1-4795-70683 (eBook PDF)
1. Senses and sensation—Juvenile literature. 2. Human physiology—Juvenile literature. I. Title.
QP434.T76 2016
612.8—dc23   2014049606

Printed in the United States of America in North Mankato, Minnesota.
032014   008087CGF14

Look for all the books in the series:

ARE BOWLING BALLS BULLIES? Learning About Forces and Motion with **THE GARBAGE GANG**

DO ANTS GET LOST? Learning About Animal Communication with **THE GARBAGE GANG**

DO BEES POOP? Learning About Living and Nonliving Things with **THE GARBAGE GANG**

DO PLANTS HAVE HEADS? Learning About Plant Parts with **THE GARBAGE GANG**

WHAT'S WITH THE LONG NAPS, BEARS? Learning About Hibernation with **THE GARBAGE GANG**

WHY DO DEAD FISH FLOAT? Learning About Matter with **THE GARBAGE GANG**

WHY DOES MY BODY MAKE BUBBLES? Learning About the Digestive System with **THE GARBAGE GANG**

YOU CALL THAT A NOSE? Learning About Human Senses with **THE GARBAGE GANG**

More books! Are you kidding me? This is the best news since sliced bread!

Seriously?